PRINCIPLES
of Faith

(Five things that Unleash Your Sixth Sense)

by

Andrew Allans Mutambo

PRINCIPLES OF FAITH

Unless otherwise noted, all scripture quotations are from the
original King James Version of the Bible.

Rivendell Publishing

www.rivendellpublishing.com

To order copies online visit:

Andrewmutambo.com

Or by mail contact:

Pastor Andrew Mutambo

P.O BOX 22292

Kampala, Uganda.

U.S (Google line): 1-804-601-0394. Ugandan

(Mobile line) : +256-772-404389 Email:

andymutts@gmail.com

Layout desgin: Elohe Enterprise Designs

Dedication

I owe everything about this book to the great King and Father of all, for the grace to write a manuscript about faith. My prayer for you all who chance to read this book is that the good Lord will awaken and stir your faith into deeper dimensions. Let the principles set forth here become a guiding factor into higher levels of life.

In addition, my parents have been my role models from a tender age. Dad has always encouraged me to go higher, while Mum has often been the soft spoken prophet in my life. Thank you, Dad and Mum, for the nurturing work you have done in me. Most of the principles you taught me are still sustaining me to this day. I dedicate this book to you as well.

Acknowledgements

To my fellow pastors' in Revived Glory Church, thank you for your continuous encouragement, love, prayers and for allowing me time to pursue this dream and its authorial formulation. And to my Church family, my sincere gratitude for your love, support and patience during the times of separation and study in the course of writing my books. You are the wind beneath my wings.

Apostle Charles Tumwine of New Life Ministries in Uganda, I commend you for always being my counselor and friend. Pastor Danny Mbako, as a longtime friend turned brother, your words of encouragement are bench marks in my life.

My sincere thanks and gratitude go to Bill Jackson, of Charlottesville, Virginia, for the time he has put in editing my manuscript.

Preface

The word faith translated from the Greek word pistis means 'persuasion, conviction, reliance on Christ, constancy in profession, assurance, belief, reliability, truthfulness of God, confidence and expectation'. Faith is the bedrock of our Christian life, the means through which we access the unseen God and the driving force behind the eternal life we so cherish in Christ Jesus. Minus faith, it is impossible to please God and access anything accruing to us as His children.

The Apostle Paul in his letters to the different churches, describes faith as a law, as our breastplate, as our righteousness, as a communication, as a profession, as a fight, as a mystery, as a work, as a shield, as a door, as words and as our sacrifice and service. His point was, when faith is tapped into and released, it manifests itself in different forms and ways. Like a diamond stone that is subjected to sunlight, its different facets automatically reflect or give off soft rays of light revealing the power and beauty of the stone!

Faith acts as our sixth sense, helping us sniff the unseen world and unlock the hidden things therein. It is the bridge between the spiritual world and the earthly realm, mortal man and the infinite God. It's the only language Heaven understands. It is the unseen force that moves God to respond to the prayers and praises of His people AND the versatile weapon that overcomes the spirit of fear which Satan uses as his greatest tool.

When we look into the ministry travels of Jesus and the miracles He performed, you will repeatedly notice His resounding words, 'your faith has made you whole'. He often said these words when encountered by desperate persons whose faith challenged Him to instantaneously act on their behalf. And all through the pages of the Bible, case scenarios of faith are projected with God's immediate response to these beckoning calls and acts.

Child of God, in this book, I approach the subject of Faith differently. I look at the principles governing Faith. Your life is a safe depository box of a Master key that unlocks life's treasures and releases the many untapped resources of the unseen world. However, knowing its application is imperative. It's one thing to have the right key but another placing it in the right locks.

Follow me through the pages of this book as I unravel the five things that unleash your sixth sense of faith. All through our chapters, we shall refer to the scriptural text below as our study guide. This verse is an embodiment of five key statements. These are going to help us discover and rightly apply this Key of faith. Let us hoist the sails and begin our expedition.

Hebrews 11:13 These all died in faith, not having received the promises, but having seen them afar off, and were persuaded of them, and embraced them, and confessed that they were strangers and pilgrims on the earth.

Table of Contents

Chapter one

FAITH SEES AFAR OFF

The book of Hebrews, which some scholars attribute to Paul, reserves a wall of fame in the eleventh chapter to the patriarchs, all of whom all died in faith, unable to visibly see and experience the New Testament promises of the coming of the Messiah and the outpouring of the Holy Spirit, but whose faith compelled them to be mindful of an Eternal City whose builder and maker is God. I want you to take note of one of the phrase in our scriptural text that says, 'but having seen them afar off'. In spite of their inability to experience firsthand the promises God's Spirit was witnessing to them, their sheer insight into the mind of God about this City gave them overwhelming hope to remain faithful during their earthly pilgrimage. Therefore, when it comes to understanding how faith works, the phrase (faith sees afar off) becomes a strong basis for our deposition. The element of 'sight' is cardinal in our Faith. Allow me say, 'faith is incomplete without sight'. Let us go a little deeper and examine this.

Abram has had a harrowing experience with his herdsmen and those of Lot his nephew. Continuous squabbles amongst their men compel him to call an abrupt family meeting to try and settle matters. He tells Lot, in essence, "As much as I would have loved to keep you with me, it is time we took our separate ways given the enormity of blessings God has given us." He tells him to choose between the left or the right side of the land. Lot opts for the plain of Jordan that is well watered and journeys East. Abram on the other hand remains in the land of Canaan. Immediately after Lot's departure, God speaks to Abram giving him specific instructions. Six things we learn from this biblical passage that help us understand how faith sees afar off.

Genesis 13:14 And the LORD said unto Abram, after that Lot was separated from him, Lift up now thine eyes, and look from the place where thou art northward, and southward, and eastward, and westward:

Genesis 13:15 For all the land which thou seest, to thee will I give it, and to thy seed for ever.

Genesis 13:16 And I will make thy seed as the dust of the earth: so that if a man can number the dust of the earth, then shall thy seed also be numbered.

Genesis 13:17 Arise, walk through the land in the length of it and in the breadth of it; for I will give it unto thee.

Genesis 13:18 Then Abram removed his tent, and came and dwelt in the plain of Mamre, which is in Hebron, and built there an altar unto the LORD.

1.   Separation.

After their departure from Ur of Chaldea, God tells Abram nothing solid until he is separated from Lot. Remember this is his nephew he has migrated with from Haran, the land of their fore-fathers. They have lived together for many years and experienced a strong brotherly bond. Breaking away from each other especially in a 'foreign land' was not going to be easy. I suspect that the bickering amongst their herdsmen had gone on for some time and that God had on several occasions told Abram it was time to move on. However, seeing his nephew grow into a man was not something easy to part with. One morning/evening, whatever time of the day it was, Abram summons the courage, calls Lot and tells him his mind.

Every one of us from the onset of our spiritual pilgrimage has a 'Lot' we are meant to separate from in order to step into the next phase of our assignment. This 'Lot' comes in different shapes and forms; attitudes, mental dispositions, temperaments, beliefs, habits, traditions, totems and people. Some of these things/persons become so attached to us over time that allowing God to 'tear' them from us requires a sizable sacrifice on our part.

The name Lot, comes from a Hebrew root word which means, 'a veil or covering'. Implying, all the time Abram was with Lot, he had a covering/veil on him that inhibited him from seeing and accessing his destined path. Child of God, before your faith can See afar off, the different veils (or call them Lots) have to be severed from you. It is time to say your good byes to those things God has been telling you about, even if it means dismissing them so that you may be able to run unencumbered the race set before you.

Hebrews 12:1 Wherefore seeing we also are compassed about with so great a cloud of witnesses, let us lay aside every weight, and the sin which doth so easily beset us, and let us run with patience the race that is set before us.

2.   Seer's eye.

The fourteenth verse tells us that once the separation has taken place, God tells Abram to lift his eyes and look. In my opinion, the sight God was referring to was the spiritual one, since the promise being made was touching his seed for generations to come. God was opening the spiritual eyes of Abram to see the future of an established Nation of Israel with a multitude of his grandchildren spread abroad across this expanse of land. Abram at that moment had to turn loose and widen his Seer's eye in order to see the future promises for him and his seed.

Friends, we all have been given a Seer's eye that is hidden in our conscience. When we come to Christ, this eye is opened and developed as we grow in the grace and knowledge of our Lord Jesus Christ. This is the eye of faith. Being spiritual beings, governed by spiritual laws and living in the earthly realm, the necessity of developing this eye to detect and prepare duly for what is ours is important. Before God releases our substances, He often allows us see them in their raw spiritual form. It is then up to us to petition and proclaim them into this realm. That is why throughout scripture, God speaks to His people saying, (Lift up your eyes and see, Behold I do a new thing—John 4:35/Isaiah 43:19) The reason being, he does not want us to miss the whole picture of what He is willing to manifest to His children through their prayers and praises. Nurturing your prophetic eye that is able to see beyond any natural barriers, through the promises (Word of God) that He has made available for you, is vital for living a fruitful and victorious life.

Jeremiah 1:11 Moreover the word of the LORD came unto me, saying, Jeremiah, what seest thou? And I said, I see a rod of an almond tree.

Jeremiah 1:12 Then said the LORD unto me, Thou hast

well seen: for I will hasten my word to perform it.

3.   Starting Point.

All our journeys of faith have a starting point. Starting points may vary depending on the spiritual, economic, social and political climate around you. At times these are evidenced by where you live. Some people are privileged to be born in peaceful and stable environments, while others grope with war, famine and disease....trying to make a living. Whatever your state of affairs, past or present, every human being is faced with mounting challenges that will always want to become their undertaker.

In our passage, Abram is told to lift his eyes from where he is, signifying a starting point in God's promises and blessings for his life. After giving up a life of comfort and being told to embark on a journey out of his ancestral home, he did not know what the future held. As he faithfully journeys, he comes to a spot where God tells him, 'from where you are standing, from this spot, from this moment on, I have this much laid up for you.'

Like Abram, if you shall faithfully embark on your kingdom journey that God is going telling you about, without a doubt He is going to start blessing you. It doesn't matter your location, background, situation, education, experience, knowledge, status, profession, age and nationality....from where you are, that is where your blessing will commence. The Chinese have an old proverb, 'every thousand mile journey begins with the first step'. Stand your ground and don't look back, your salvation is on the way.

Deuteronomy 9:1 Hear, O Israel: Thou art to pass over Jordan this day, to go in to possess nations greater and mightier than thyself, cities great and fenced up to heaven,

Deuteronomy 9:2 A people great and tall, the children of the Anakims, whom thou knowest, and of whom thou hast heard say, Who can stand before the children of Anak!

Deuteronomy 9:3 Understand therefore this day, that the LORD thy God is he which goeth over before thee;

as a consuming fire he shall destroy them, and he shall bring them down before thy face: so shalt thou drive them out, and destroy them quickly, as the LORD hath said unto thee.

Deuteronomy 9:4 Speak not thou in thine heart, after that the LORD thy God hath cast them out from before thee, saying, For my righteousness the LORD hath brought me in to possess this land: but for the wickedness of these nations the LORD doth drive them out from before thee.

Deuteronomy 9:5 Not for thy righteousness, or for the uprightness of thine heart, dost thou go to possess their land: but for the wickedness of these nations the LORD thy God doth drive them out from before thee, and that he may perform the word which the LORD sware unto thy fathers, Abraham, Isaac, and Jacob.

4.   Selection.

God continues his conversation with Abram, telling him to look north, south, east and west; in all four directions.

Do you know why He told him this? It is because God's blessings to him were without measure. In essence, God was telling Abram that the measure you receive is going to depend on the measure you behold. When God shows or tells you something, He has more in mind than your finite mind can comprehend. That is why it is vital in those moments when He is giving you a 'virtual reality tour' of your dreams, to try and see the big picture through His divine eyes. This will put you on the same page with Him.

Additionally, the four directions speak of the options and opportunities God has for you. There are countless doors He is able to fling open, so stop focusing on a particular one. The four directions are God's hidden statement to you that hey! I am able and willing to bless you from any angle and direction so be on the lookout!

Proverbs 23:7 For as he thinketh in his heart, so is he: Eat and drink, saith he to thee; but his heart is not with thee.

Mathew 8:13 And Jesus said unto the centurion, Go thy

way; and as thou hast believed, so be it done unto thee. And his servant was healed in the selfsame hour.

5.   Survey.

After Abram looks at the vast opportunities and blessings surrounding him, he is told to survey his domain, I mean walk through it. He begins the task of spiritual mapping....for those who understand the language of spiritual warfare. He begins marking his territory like a male lion does to wade off any intruders. In Abram's case, he begins walking through the length and breadth of the land prophesying and speaking the promise of God into being. While doing so, he pictures everything falling into place and becoming what God has told him, a father of many nations.

Like Abraham your father of faith, it is time you began walking the length and breadth of your promises. Is it a building facility, a piece of property, your health, a job, a marriage? Take time on a continuous basis to spiritually survey and map out your domain. If you cannot access it physically, use that dream/vision that God has shown you as the platform to tread its breadth and length.

However, if it is within reach, then take an onsite survey and walk around its parameters.

Following this pattern systematically is going to help you fortify and seal **the aspect of sight in your faith**. Folks, it marvels me seeing a Canaanite woman engaging Jesus and receiving from Him a miracle, 'food that was meant for the children', because she defied the odds, left home after having walked around her demon vexed child saying, 'today you are going to be delivered even if you are a non-Jew.'

Mat 15:21 Then Jesus went thence, and departed into the coasts of Tyre and Sidon.

Mat 15:22 And, behold, a woman of Canaan came out of the same coasts, and cried unto him, saying, Have mercy on me, O Lord, thou Son of David; my daughter is grievously vexed with a devil.

Mat 15:23 But he answered her not a word. And his disciples came and besought him, saying, Send her away; for she crieth after us.

Mat 15:24 But he answered and said, I am not sent but unto the lost sheep of the house of Israel.

Mat 15:25 Then came she and worshipped him, saying, Lord, help me.

Mat 15:26 But he answered and said, It is not meet to take the children's bread, and to cast it to dogs.

Mat 15:27 And she said, Truth, Lord: yet the dogs eat of the crumbs which fall from their masters' table.

Mat 15:28 Then Jesus answered and said unto her, O woman, great is thy faith: be it unto thee even as thou wilt. And her daughter was made whole from that very hour.

6.   Station

In concluding our first chapter, we notice that God is done speaking to Abram and showing him his destiny. Abram dismantles his tent and moves from his place of abode to Hebron. The word Hebron comes from a Hebrew root word meaning, 'a seat of association, associate, companion, fellow'. When your **faith begins seeing afar off**, you purposely and perceptively shift your spiritual abode from your current location to the 'place' you are meant to be. Abram's eyes were opened and he moved into a new dimension of associations, connections and companionship, God leading him to rub shoulders with the great men of the land (Hebron).

In a similar manner, God wants you to shift your spiritual focus from where you are and begin seeing yourself in that place of excellence, prosperity, health and greatness. Time to break camp, shift your mental disposition and see yourself living in your cherished God-given dreams. Luke 12:34 For where your treasure is, there will your heart be also.

Joshua 1:3 Every place that the sole of your foot shall tread upon, that have I given unto you, as I said unto Moses.
Joshua 1:4 From the wilderness and this Lebanon even unto the great river, the river Euphrates, all the land of the Hittites, and unto the great sea toward the going down of the sun, shall be your coast.

Chapter Two

FAITH IS FULLY PERSUADED

In this chapter, we quote another statement in our Hebrews study guide, 'and were persuaded of them' (Hebrews 11:13). The patriarchs died persuaded there was an Eternal City they would one day live in. It made their hearts rest in full assurance of their hope. The word persuaded means, 'convinced, certain, absolutely sure and content'. After their Seer's eye had peered into the invisible realm and beheld the future promises, they automatically became convinced, certain, absolutely sure and content about their visions.

This phrase teaches us another principle, that your faith ought to be persuaded about what it sees. Seeing is only a starter. Walking through the steps I have shared in the preceding chapter puts you in line for your next step, which is persuasion. How can one be persuaded, that is, convinced, certain, absolutely sure and content about what they are seeing? Let us dissect the following texts for answers.

Romans 4:17 As it is written, I have made thee a father of many nations, before him whom he believed, even God, who quickeneth the dead, and calleth those things which be not as though they were.

Romans 4:18 Who against hope believed in hope, that he might become the father of many nations, according to that which was spoken, So shall thy seed be.

Romans 4:19 And being not weak in faith, he considered not his own body now dead, when he was about an hundred years old, neither yet the deadness of Sara's womb:

Romans 4:20 He staggered not at the promise of God through unbelief; but was strong in faith, giving glory to God;

Romans 4:21 And being fully persuaded that, what he had promised, he was able also to perform.

Romans 4:22 And therefore it was imputed to him for righteousness.

Romans 4:23 Now it was not written for his sake alone, that it was imputed to him;

Romans 4:24 But for us also, to whom it shall be imputed, if we believe on him that raised up Jesus our Lord from the dead;

Romans 4:25 Who was delivered for our offences, and was raised again for our justification.

Paul has written to the church in Rome telling them that justification in Christ comes by grace through faith and not by the works of the law. In this chapter, he uses Abraham their forefather as the best example and clearly points out that even he was not justified by works, but by his faith.

There are five things in this biblical passage that help us understand how Persuasion of faith comes about:

1. Canonical consciousness.

In verse seventeen, Abraham was nearly clocking 100 years and still without an heir. His strong attachment to the supremacy of God's oath and promise spoken to him at the outset of his pilgrimage, created a recurring consciousness of the reality and truthfulness of God, even when faced with a situation as dire as his. In the pursuit of our dreams, and despite the delays associated with them, our continuous hinging on God's promises will create a consciousness that will help bring absolute certainty and contentment to us.

2. Contrary to circumstances.

Abraham's persuasion was fueled by a hope that goes beyond the natural one. On the face of it, his body and that of Sarah, were beyond child bearing stage; but he refused to yield to the fading hope and rather chose to be governed by a higher law, a spiritual one that works contrary to the natural laws and circumstances of life. This law is put into effect by the Word of God. The word of God is the well spring of God's promises and faith. You and I can go contrary to the laws of life only if we decide to reach for a higher law, the law of faith. It is said that water boils at 100 C or 212 F. However, if you add a pinch of salt to it, the boiling point rises to 102 C or 216 F. Why, because you introduced a higher law to the ordinary one. By the same token, we go contrary to the laws of life when we switch gears from natural hope to the spiritual hope.

3.   Consideration.

A further look at the passage reveals another pillar of 'persuasion' called consideration. Consideration says, 'there is still a way out'. The ninetieth verse declares that he considered not his body dead neither the deadness of Sarah's womb but kept reflecting on and contemplating the promise of fathering many nations. He drew a positive out of a negative situation. He went scuba diving beneath his frail body, past the feelings and dictates of his flesh to excavate the hidden promises that had been buried for the last twenty-five years. When he was again afloat, what was on the surface no longer mattered because of his persuasion. It changed his consideration, because he saw a way out. What keeps this confident consideration strong is our continuous reflection on the promises.

4.   Contain-ability.

The twentieth verse goes on to say that Abraham did not stagger at the promise but was strong in faith. What gave him stamina and strength in the face of overwhelming odds, was the persuasion 'to hold on and hold out.' Persuasion creates an internal circular flow of spiritual energy, somewhat like a mini-twister or whirlwind. The more Abraham was persuaded (convinced, certain, absolutely sure) about God's promises, the more this internal flow of spiritual energy grew in him. He was able to contain it to levels where his faith became strong with every passing day. Likewise, our ability to stand tall amidst the crushing weight of satanic opposition lies in our storage capacity. Seeing to it that there is no leakage or passing out of this spiritual current contained within, but harnessing it till it generates more and more faith power.

5.   Celebrates.

Persuasion brought him to a place where he began giving thanks and glory to God in every passing day. He ignored what his mind and body were saying, and held hard and fast to the absoluteness of God's promises. For this he was declared righteous before God and received the title 'father of faith'. When persuasion fills your heart, it creates an atmosphere of thanksgiving. Since you are now convinced and absolutely sure that it is a done deal, you put on your dancing shoes and begin celebrating God for what He is going to do. Folks, these five indicators are mandatory in our Persuasion, a second important principle of faith!

Chapter Three
FAITH ALWAYS EMBRACES

As we continue our discussion, I am steadily building my case for the principles governing faith. In this chapter, I focus on another phrase, 'and embraced them' (Hebrews 11:13), referring to the patriarchs who were mindful of the Eternal City. What did they embrace? The scripture says they embraced the promises. How did they do that? Well, let us first examine the word 'embrace'. Embrace is taken from a Hebrew root word meaning, 'to clasp, fold, welcome.' The implication is that after seeing the promises from afar and being fully persuaded (convinced) about them, they welcomed, folded and clasped them into their bosoms. Another principle is faith always embraces!

The ability to enfold and clasp what you believe and not let go. We all know that when you embrace someone, you literally wrap your arms around them, hold them tight, feel their heart-beat, experience their warmth and love

AND in some instances don't want to let them go. In the same manner, the patriarchs embraced the promises and felt 'their' overwhelming reality within and around them.

Scripture will always back up scripture. The book of Genesis documents a story that can help throw more light on the embrace factor.

Genesis 19:1 And there came two angels to Sodom at even; and Lot sat in the gate of Sodom: and Lot seeing them rose up to meet them; and he bowed himself with his face toward the ground;

Genesis 19:2 And he said, Behold now, my lords, turn in, I pray you, into your servant's house, and tarry all night, and wash your feet, and ye shall rise up early, and go on your ways. And they said, Nay; but we will abide in the street all night.

Genesis 19:3 And he pressed upon them greatly; and they turned in unto him, and entered into his house; and he made them a feast, and did bake unleavened bread, and they did eat.

Lot is coming up again in our discussion, this time not as a culprit, but as an activist. He is seated in the gate of Sodom making silent intercession over a City he sees descending into moral decadency. His perceptive eye catches two men striding towards the City who he knew were not of Sodom. And knowing the consequence that would befall them if not attended to, he decides to show them hospitality. Notice the steps he took from the start:

1.   Discerns.

When he sees the angels coming towards the gate of Sodom, he quickly rises to meet them. Lot was cognizant of the timing and opportunity that was before hand. This ties into what we have already discussed about faith seeing afar off, but this time, not sitting back and acknowledging it from a distance. There was response and effort on the part of Lot. He met them half way. The same thing is required of us by God when He releases His promises to us. Our response should be rising from our fear, frustration, prayers and praises to do the needful. It is one thing to dream and keep dreaming like many folks do AND it is another to discern and walk towards our dreams.

2.   Draws.

The passage goes on to say that when the encounter takes place, he begins drawing them. He implores them to turn into his house. For a while, they act as though they would not. His persistence and insistence pays off and they accept his invitation) to come into his house. The same goes with us when we try to clasp and welcome the promises of God into our lives. This time it is the enemy (devil) who mounts spiritual resistance and tries to hustle and wrestle the promises from making entrance. The forces of fear, anxiety, negativity, doubt, self pity, unbelief and ignorance do their best to foil and hinder us. But notice, Lot clings to these angels till they accept.

3.   Detains.

After that duel, his next assignment is to detain them or have them settle in the house for a night before they embark on their journey the following morning. Like Lot, prepare and position your heart to feel and experience the promises that are in your reach. It doesn't matter what your mind or body is saying, go with that inner feeling. Let them (promises) abide with you for the 'night'. Night is symbolic of those lonely and unclear seasons in time when you definitely need the promises for comfort, uplifting and nourishment till the 'morning time' of their fruition comes. When these promises are detained they become a protection by guarding your destiny.

4.   Dresses.

The guests are now in the house, have had their feet washed as the custom was and are whetting their appetite for the best meal and room service they would envisage in Sodom. Lot prepares them a feast, baking for them unleavened bread. The promises of God would love to settle in a 'house', that is, your heart that is open and ready for them. When our faith is cognizant of God's promises and becomes persuaded that they are a 'Yes and Amen factor', we begin to wholly embrace them by demonstrating a wholesome fondness for them. This involves intense fellowship and communion with them. This will steadily metamorphose them and before you realize it, they will have become a reality. I reiterate, embrace is another key principle in our faith!

Chapter Four

FAITH ALWAYS CONFESSES

The patriarchs went on to confess that they were strangers and pilgrims on the earth. What a remarkable statement! They were not going to be blinded by the present glory or succumb to the current sufferings. They let their faith bellow out what they had embraced, 'we are only passing through, weeping may endure for the night but joy surely comes in the morning, this sickness is only for a while, this financial situation will surely pass'. They were optimistic about the 'dawning of a new day' when life's tears, fears and snares would be no more. Folks, the confession of our faith is another landmark in the pursuit of our promises and their eventual fulfillment.

The story of David and Goliath has always been a fascinating tale in the Children's church. And for the adult Christian, it offers diverse lessons depending on one's mode of approach.

1 Samuel 17:32 And David said to Saul, Let no man's heart fail because of him; thy servant will go and fight with this Philistine.

1 Samuel 17:33 And Saul said to David, Thou art not able to go against this Philistine to fight with him: for thou art but a youth, and he a man of war from his youth.

1 Samuel 17:34 And David said unto Saul, Thy servant kept his father's sheep, and there came a lion, and a bear, and took a lamb out of the flock:

1 Samuel 17:35 And I went out after him, and smote him, and delivered it out of his mouth: and when he arose against me, I caught him by his beard, and smote him, and slew him.

1 Samuel 17:36 Thy servant slew both the lion and the bear: and this uncircumcised Philistine shall be as one of them, seeing he hath defied the armies of the living God.

1 Samuel 17:37 David said moreover, The LORD that delivered me out of the paw of the lion, and out of the

paw of the bear, he will deliver me out of the hand of this Philistine. And Saul said unto David, Go, and the LORD be with thee.

1 Samuel 17:38 And Saul armed David with his armour, and he put an helmet of brass upon his head; also he armed him with a coat of mail.

1 Samuel 17:39 And David girded his sword upon his armour, and he assayed to go; for he had not proved it. And David said unto Saul, I cannot go with these; for I have not proved them. And David put them off him.

1 Samuel 17:40 And he took his staff in his hand, and chose him five smooth stones out of the brook, and put them in a shepherd's bag which he had, even in a scrip; and his sling was in his hand: and he drew near to the Philistine.

At this stage in our passage, David who is only meant to take food for his elder brothers arrives at the battle scene and from a distance hears Goliath taunting the armies of Israel. Out of curiosity, he decides to venture a little farther onto the battle lines, after leaving the food with the provisions officer. He stumbles on a group of soldiers who are scared to death of Goliath but verbally fantasizing about King Saul's rewards to the Man who will slay him. He interrupts their conversation by asking for clarity about the rewards to be given to the slayer. His inquisition falls into the ears of King Saul and David is speedily summoned. He goes to on to tell the King, 'I will go and fight with this Philistine'. Five viable lessons from this passage underscore the principle of confession in faith.

1.   Positive.

The thirty second verse begins with an emphatic statement by David, 'I will go and fight this Philistine. His public declaration amidst a strong prevailing wind of fear is meant to reverse the negative trend of words the nine foot giant is using to control the minds of the armies of Israel. His words to the King are packed with self belief and confidence. Saints, being positive is a crucial ingredient in the recipe of Confession. It is one thing to utter words with a positive tone, but it is another when the positivity saturates your heart. It makes your words powerful and effective. Confession is the outflow of the heart's disposition.

2.   Pervert.

Notice in the thirty third verse that when David tries to alter the psychological climate on the battle field, he receives a 'slap in the face'. The words of Saul contrasting the lad's inexperience with the experience of his adversary come against David's fiery zeal and passion. It is a calculated ploy of the enemy (devil) to divert David from his positive confession by making him focus on his size and years of experience. However, it is to no avail. David sticks to his guns. I advise you, my dear friend, to always watch out for those voices of dissuasion and discouragement whenever you try to take a stand against your 'Goliath'.

3.   Ponder.

The negative speech by King Saul was quickly and vehemently counteracted by a statement of fact from David. In his defense, David pulls out his life's journal and begins rehearsing before the King and his officers what transpired during his tenure as a Shepherd boy in the fields. How at one time a bear and a lion came and tried to take lambs out of his flock. He responded swiftly by attacking them and delivering the innocent lambs out of their jaws. David then relates his victorious experience over these beasts to Goliath. The gist is, he allowed his faith to 'loudly ponder' his past victories which marked him as the right candidate for the mission to kill Goliath. Did you know that the word, 'meditate', in the Bible actually means 'to mumble, to mutter?' In the course of David's pondering, he was actually meditating on God's faithfulness and mighty hand of triumph during those battles. Begin pondering/meditating on your past victories and let yourself be catapulted to your next level.

4.   Presume.

After Saul is outwitted by David's speech and charisma, he opts to provide David with the necessary gear, since his dress is not suited for the battlefield. Saul is doing this with good intention because he sees this young lad vulnerable before the weaponry of this mammoth warrior. David tries it on but is unable to find mobility and balance. He declines the offer and chooses to face the enemy without armor with the tools he feels led of

God to use.

This teaches us that we may learn from others but should not copy their styles. Every spiritual battle we face has its designated weapons. At times, our confession may be packaged in songs of praises, direct quoting of the holy scriptures, recitation of hymns OR a prayer of petition.

God helps us to stand tall when we learn to voice our faith through confession. It is not the scriptures we quote, but the inspiration we derive from them that grants us power to demolish our foes. Never presume that what works for others may work for you. Remember, your confession is simply the outflow and overflow of the promises you have embraced. In reality, you are voicing what you are experiencing in the inside of you. And that is what David did!

5. Propels.

Confession is a supernatural force that systematically advances you through enemy lines to your victory as you keep decreeing the promises in and out of season over your situation. David's pronunciations propelled him beyond familiar territory into enemy lines, and each step of faith was a symbol of registered victory. The fortieth verse says that he took his sling after choosing five smooth stones from the stream. He came within reasonable hurling distance and delivered a fatal blow to his enemy. Goliath bites the dust as he falls like a ton of bricks face first. What a resounding victory this was. What a day to remember in that generation's calendar! Hebrews 10:23 Let us hold fast the profession of our faith without wavering; for he is faithful that promised.

Chapter Five

FAITH RECEIVES THE PROMISES

All through the preceding chapters, we have gleaned from our study text (Hebrews 11:13) while referring to the biblical patriarchs whose belief in an Eternal City was sustained by its governing principles which they upheld. Seeing that the forerunner, Christ Jesus had not yet come and prepared the way, they all died in faith not having received the promises. Notwithstanding, through His death and resurrection, these promises became accessible to them. That is why after His resurrection, many saints who had died were seen walking in the streets of Jerusalem. And for every one of us who accepts the Lordship and Kingship of Christ Jesus, there is assurance of passage (after death) into this Eternal City. Let us take a few steps back and recite our Hebrews text. It says, 'these all died in faith, not having received the promises...' Notice the word promises. Meaning, there are diverse promises that accrue to us as God's children, spiritual, physical, financial, marital, material and on. A good number of these are made available in this life, others in the life to come. Wherever and whenever, the point is, 'faith receives the promises'.

This is the last principle of faith I would like to share with you. Faith always meets its goal and fulfills its intended purpose. For whatever reason you are exercising your faith in God, be assured of tangible results.

Our story today is about a poor widow and an unjust Judge.

Luke 18:1 And he spake a parable unto them to this end, that men ought always to pray, and not to faint;

Luke 18:2 Saying, There was in a city a judge, which feared not God, neither regarded man:

Luke 18:3 And there was a widow in that city; and she came unto him, saying, Avenge me of mine adversary.

Luke 18:4 And he would not for a while: but afterward he said within himself, Though I fear not God, nor regard man;

Luke 18:5 Yet because this widow troubleth me, I will avenge her, lest by her continual coming she weary me.

Luke 18:6 And the Lord said, Hear what the unjust judge saith.

Luke 18:7 And shall not God avenge his own elect, which cry day and night unto him, though he bear long with them?

Luke 18:8 I tell you that he will avenge them speedily. Nevertheless when the Son of man cometh, shall he find faith on the earth?

Jesus in talking to his audience drives home an important lesson, the significance of faith in our Christian life. Four things handpicked from his teaching can help us understand how faith receives the promises.

1.   Supplication.

Jesus begins his parable by emphasizing the importance of prayer. He underscores the necessity of making it an integral part of one's life. As Christians, prayer is our means of fellowship and communication with God. It is the way we connect with the Eternal Being, the Creator of the universe. In this way our faith is refueled and energized as it feeds off the energy coming from the divine source. Through prayer, faith is tested, perfected and rewarded. Every one of us ought to make prayer a daily habit seeing that it is the avenue faith uses to obtain its purpose.

2.   Concept.

Jesus continues His narration talking about an unjust Judge whose notion was, 'I don't fear God neither do I respect any man.' He was an arrogant and myopic character. (Unfortunately for the residents of that City, he may have been the only judge there. Given his conception of God and man, his court rulings must have been unfair and without bail. Jesus uses the unjust judge's disposition to draw a contrast between him and the Judge of all the earth, a merciful and gracious God who in spite of our overwhelming odds, rules in our favor. When we conceptualize God in our prayers, do we see him as a stereotyped and mean spirited being? Our God is a merciful, loving and caring father who is always ready to listen and act on the prayers of his children when they approach Him in faith and righteousness. It is important to have the right conception of God when approaching him.

3. Case.

We are also told that there was a widow in that City, who has a troubling case. From the look of things she does not have the money to hire a lawyer, and there are no Pro bonos (free legal services) available. The fact that she has a serious matter requiring urgent attention, drives her to the judge's courtroom. It is a do or die situation for her. Similarly, in our pursuit of God's promises, our age-long adversary, the devil, is always out to oppose and put insurmountable barriers in our way. Nevertheless, our 'cases' are reason enough to come boldly before the throne of grace and justice, to find mercy and help in time of need. My sister and brother, you ought to have a strong case about your health, family, job, etc. that will propel you before the great throne of justice.

Isaiah 41:21 Produce your cause, saith the LORD; bring forth your strong reasons, saith the King of Jacob.

4.   Consistency.

Each time this widow goes to the judge to have her petition heard, her case is dismissed. She does not throw in the towel. She returns home, dusts herself off and returns to the courtroom to lodge her appeal afresh. The judge becomes annoyed and weary of her presence and plea. He is convinced that if this widow keeps this vigil, he will be drained. That night, he makes up his mind to rule in her favor and the following day on his way to his chambers, asks his secretary for her file.

Her consistency and persistence pays off, the scales have tipped in her favor. The secretary, astonished, signals to the widow that this is a good sign. Long story short, the case is heard and ruled in her favor. A valuable lesson for every Christian that we ought to keep asking, seeking and knocking until we are in receipt of our promises. Remember in our introduction, we see Paul characterizing faith as a fight! There are promises that we have to stand up for. They may take us long seasons of consistence and persistence, but we have to be up to the challenge. God is faithful to bring to pass what He has promised.

5.   Composed.

After a long struggle, her faith is rewarded. The passage does not tell us the duration she had to bear with this ordeal. She storms out of the courtroom that has become her second home, leaping and shouting for joy. This time the minority has prevailed. The victim has become a victor. Her story hits the morning and evening news of the market place and 'water- spots' where women went in the evenings to draw water. She is the talk of town, the sensation of the City. She is reaping the benefits of her fervent faith through petition (prayer).

She has steadfastly clung onto her conviction that, 'this will surely work out, I am not sure how, but it doubtless will'. Look at the immense rewards of a patient seeker who never gives up in spite of the 'seeming silence' and passive response of our God. Someone willing to fight for his/her territory while stuck in the 'trenches' of the scripture that says, 'He knows the way that I take and when He has tried me, I shall come forth as gold'. Such a one, who is unwilling to surrender any inch or iota of their God given promises to Satan. This, my friend, is the mark of faith. It is my earnest prayer for you that

God will fulfill all His promises regarding your life and keep your head above the waters in the process. Our final principle is....faith receives the promises!

Conclusion

I am so thankful to God for the Men and Women of Old whose lives have been a yard stick and example of our faith. We do well to learn and identify with their strengths, weaknesses and above all their tenacity in pursuit of destiny. The holy scriptures tell us that "through faith they subdued kingdoms, wrought righteousness, obtained promises, stopped the mouths of lions, quenched the violence of fire, escaped the edge of the sword, out of weakness were made strong, waxed valiant in fight, turned to flight the armies of the aliens, women received their dead raised to life again: and others were tortured, not accepting deliverance; that they might obtain a better resurrection. And others had trial of cruel mocking and scourging, yea, moreover of bonds and imprisonment. They were stoned, they were sawn asunder, were tempted, were slain with the sword: they wandered about in sheepskins and goatskins; being destitute, afflicted, tormented; (of whom the world was not worthy). They wandered in deserts, and in mountains, and in dens and caves of the earth. And these all, having obtained a good report through faith, received not the promise: God having provided some better thing for us, that they without us should not be made perfect." (Hebrews 11: 33-40).

Friends, God purposed that they would not attain the object of their faith without us. Thank God for sending Jesus! You should therefore be inspired and fueled with the belief that He who began the good work in you will accomplish it. God is a starter and a finisher. When he created the heavens and the earth, he was done on the sixth day and rested on the seventh. In His salvation plan for man, after fulfilling all requirements He cried, "It is finished."

As God's masterpieces, the manuals (plans) for our lives have already been written. When we begin the salvation walk, each of us endeavors to discover the contents of our manuals and live them to the fullest. Many a time the different segments of these manuals are like riddles, often unclear and hard to interpret, requiring our sixth sense of faith to navigate through them with ease and precision. Folks, without faith it is impossible to please

God. I encourage you to discover your manual from the mega manual (Bible) that catalogs everything about life. When you do, the principles of faith will become a meaningful adventure for you. I wish you God speed as you embark on the epic journey of faith, guided by its principles which are sure to lead you 'home'. God bless.

Other Books written by Andrew Allans Mutambo:

1. Four Faces of a Worshipper.
2. Worship Keys for Worth-full Living.
3. Gates of Worship.
4. Purpose of praise.
5. Principles of Faith.

Coming Soon:

1. Dynamics of God's word.
2. Seven Significances of the Cross.
3. Nine Elements of Worship.
4. Composition of Worship.
5. Seven Locks of the Anointing.
6. Seven Characteristics of Prayer.